Becoming a Butterfly

Krysia Kij

Rosen Classroom Books and Materials
New York

A butterfly does not begin life as a butterfly.

A butterfly begins life as a caterpillar.

3

egg

A caterpillar begins life as a tiny egg.

4

The egg breaks open and a caterpillar crawls out.

The caterpillar eats a lot of green leaves.

6

The caterpillar grows bigger.
Soon, it grows out of its skin.

The caterpillar makes a hard shell.

8

The caterpillar changes into a butterfly inside the shell.

9

Then the butterfly breaks out of the shell.

The butterfly spreads its wings and flies away!

11

Words to Know

butterfly

caterpillar

egg

leaves

wings